Fresh & Fun

April

BY JACQUELINE CLARKE

SCHOLASTIC
PROFESSIONAL BOOKS

NEW YORK • TORONTO • LONDON • AUCKLAND • SYDNEY
MEXICO CITY • NEW DELHI • HONG KONG

For my mother, whose life began in April

Firefly riddle, page 16. Reprinted with permission of Margaret K. McElderry Books, an imprint of Simon & Schuster Children's Publishing Division from RIDDLE ROAD by Elizabeth Spires. Text copyright © 1999 by Elizabeth Spires.

"I'm a Little Chicken" by Susan Peters from HOLIDAY PIGGYBACK SONGS.
Copyright © 1988 by Warren Publishing House. Used by permission of the publisher.

"Poetry Time" copyright © 1992 by Lee Bennett Hopkins. Reprinted by permission of Curtis Brown Ltd.

"Poets Go Wishing" by Lilian Moore. Copyright © 1975 by Lilian Moore.
Used by permission of Marian Reiner for the author.

"Who Am I?" from AT THE TOP OF MY VOICE AND OTHER POEMS by Felice Holman.
Copyright © 1971 by Felice Holman. Published by Charles Scribner's Sons. Reprinted by permission of the author.

Produced by Joan Novelli
Front cover, interior, and poster design by Kathy Massaro
Cover and interior art by Shelley Dieterichs
Poster art by Liisa Chauncy Guida

ISBN 0-439-21608-7
Copyright © 2000 by Jacqueline Clarke
Printed in the U.S.A.
All rights reserved.

Contents

About This Book

April is a busy month! Spring cleaning, science fairs, sports practices, parent-teacher conferences…the list goes on and on. Yet, there are some wonderful events and seasonal changes that beg to be celebrated.

This book brings you creative activities for teaching with four favorite spring themes and topics. NATIONAL POETRY MONTH invites us to discover a new favorite poem or even the poet within! EARTH DAY encourages us to show appreciation for the plants and animals that share our world. RAIN AND THE WATER CYCLE may keep us indoors, but they also teach us about rain and the water cycle. Finally, EGGS, as a symbol of new life, remind us of how we continue to grow and change.

Many of the activities were contributed by teachers across the country, giving you a glimpse of what's going on in their classrooms during the month of April. Activities cover all areas of the curriculum, many naturally integrating more than one subject.

Here's what else you'll find:

- a reproducible send-home activity calendar
- a rhyming mini-play
- literature connections
- pocket chart poetry
- a reproducible mini-book
- hands-on math and science activities
- experiments
- a colorful, pull-out poetry poster with week-by-week teaching ideas
- collaborative books
- a collaborative banner
- computer connections
- poems and "piggyback" songs
- movement activities
- and more!

Throughout this book, you'll find web site suggestions to support various activities. Please remember that Internet locations and contents can change over time. We cannot guarantee the availability of sites recommended in this book at the time of publication.

Multiple Intelligences Connections

Your students learn in different ways—some are more verbal, others prefer written expression. Some are comfortable working in groups, others like independent projects. Some children's strengths lie in music, art, and other modes of expression. To help you meet your students' needs and encourage all of their strengths, you'll find all these learning modalities woven into the activities in this book.

Name _____

April Activity Calendar

Choose _____ activities to do each week this month.
Ask an adult in your family to initial the square in the box of each activity
you complete. Bring this paper back to school on _____ .

Monday	Tuesday	Wednesday	Thursday	Friday
Write the word *April* on a sheet of paper. Cut apart the letters. Make new words!	Ask someone to tell you a joke. Tell someone you know a joke.	Look at this ladybug. Find a matching ladybug on this page.	April is the fourth month of the year. Name the third month. Name the fifth month.	What do you think "It's raining cats and dogs" means? What are other ways to describe rain?
Use your hands to make the sound of rain. Slide your palms back and forth, tap and snap your fingers, clap your hands.	Pretend you're an earthworm. Show how you move. What words describe how you move?	Go outside with an adult in your family. Look at clouds. Tell each other about a picture the clouds make.	List the foods you ate today. List the fruits. List the vegetables.	Estimate how long it will take you to get ready for bed. Have someone time you.
Tell someone at home a story about your day. Include a beginning, a middle, and an end.	Make a picture time line of your day. Show what happened first, next, and so on.	Close your eyes. What sounds do you hear? See if you can name ten.	Ask a family member five questions about him- or herself. Use the answers to write a story or poem about that person.	Circle the dates for each Monday on a calendar this month. What pattern do the numbers make?
Look for signs of spring around you. Record your observations in a picture.	Look for weather information in a newspaper. List words that describe weather.	Compare yourself to someone in your family. Tell how you are alike. Tell how you are different.	Look at the words on this calendar. Can you find two that rhyme with *cake*?	Turn *April* into a tongue twister! Make up a sentence using as many words as you can that start with *a*.

Fresh & Fun April   Scholastic Professional Books

5

Computer Connection

Many organizations will allow you to sponsor an endangered animal for a small donation. In return, they'll send a packet of information about the animal. For a list of links visit

http://geocities. com/Heartland/ Farm/5353/ endg.html

Tip

If possible, locate a stuffed version of your endangered animal and let students vote on a name.

Book Break

Endangered Animals
by Faith McNulty (Scholastic, 1996)

This book provides a great introduction to this topic. In simple terms it explains how some animals become endangered and some become extinct. An invitation at the end of the book encourages children to think not only of their needs, but of those with whom they share the planet.

SCIENCE, LANGUAGE ARTS

Endangered Animal Scrapbook

Looking for a class pet to adopt? How about an endangered animal? After reading about several, let children vote on one to study. Create a scrapbook to display the information students gather. Encourage them to find and record the following:

◎ the animal's classification (mammal, reptile, etc.)

◎ drawings and/or photographs of the animal

◎ maps illustrating where the animal can be found

◎ reasons why the animal is endangered

◎ products made from the animal

◎ population statistics

◎ conservation efforts

◎ related newspaper and/or magazine articles

Let students take turns sharing their scrapbook with other classes to build awareness in your school.

Book Break

The Earth Is Painted Green: A Garden of Poems About Our Planet
edited by Barbara Brenner (Scholastic, 1994)

This wonderful collection of nearly 100 poems will encourage children to explore and appreciate nature!

Where Does All the Garbage Go?

by Melvin Berger (Newbridge Communications, 1992)

Using photographs and simple text, this book explores the different possibilities for garbage disposal including dumping, recycling, composting, and burning.

Teacher Share

MATH

Trash Basket for a Day

It is estimated that each American generates more than four pounds of trash per day. Make children aware of just how much trash they produce daily by inviting them to carry their trash with them.

Ask each child to come to school wearing a pair of pants with belt loops and to bring a plastic grocery bag with handles. Assist children in tying the handles of the bag to one of their belt loops. As children go through the day, ask them to throw any nonfood garbage into their bags. Encourage them to continue doing this in the evening while at home. The next day have children bring their trash bags back to school. Let each child weigh his or her bag of garbage. Create a graph to show how much garbage each child produced. Discuss the data: *Who produced the most garbage? Who produced the least? Was the average close to four pounds?*

Bobbie Williams
Brookwood Elementary
Snellville, Georgia

TIP

Help children learn more about the problem of trash by sorting the contents of the classroom wastebasket into four groups: Recycle, Reduce (items to use less of), Reuse (items to use again or turn into something new), and Reject (could replace with more environmentally sound products). Repeat the activity the next day. Ask: *Was there less trash in the basket than the day before?* Have students share ways they were able to cut down on the amount of garbage that went into the wastebasket.

Hey! Get Off Our Train

by John Burningham (Crown Publications, 1999)

A boy and his dog take an imaginary journey on a train. At each stop they meet an endangered animal looking to be rescued. This is a great book for children to act out. Create a train by lining up boxes or chairs, and let children take turns being one of the endangered animals, the boy, or the dog.

SCIENCE, LANGUAGE ARTS

Going, Going, Gone

As children play this variation of Duck, Duck, Goose, they will learn the difference between the terms *threatened, endangered*, and *extinct*.

◎ Gather children in a circle on the floor. Tell them they are a species or group of animals called the "Foo Foos."

◎ Walk around the circle tapping each Foo Foo on the head while saying, "going, going, gone." Each Foo Foo that is tapped on the word "gone" must leave the circle.

◎ When approximately one half of the species has "disappeared," explain that the Foo Foos are now *threatened*.

◎ Continue playing until about one half of the remaining Foo Foos have left the circle, leaving approximately one quarter of the original group. Tell children that the species is now *endangered*.

◎ Resume action until all Foo Foos have disappeared, making them an *extinct* species.

◎ Follow up with a discussion on how animals become threatened, endangered, and extinct. Ask children to suggest ways they could make a difference.

SCIENCE, SOCIAL STUDIES

Friends of the Earth

Rachel Carson was a good friend to the Earth! Work with children to find out why this was true. Create a chart listing the many ways she cared for the Earth. (For suggested resources, see Book Break, page 9, and Computer Connection, left.)

Using her life as an example, encourage children to become "Friends of the Earth." Create a large flower and staple all but the petals to a bulletin board. Paste a photo or drawing of each child in the center of the flower and title the display "Friends of the Earth." Each time a student does something to help Earth, such as picking up litter or planting a seed, record it on a petal along with his or her name and add it to the flower. Soon your flower will be blooming with environmentally friendly deeds!

Computer Connection

Check this web site for book lists, a biography, and other information about Rachel Carson:

www.rachel carson.org

Book Break

Rachel Carson: Friend of Nature
by Carol Greene (Children's Press, 1992)

This book describes the life and work of this environmentally conscious biologist and writer.

Teacher Share

LANGUAGE ARTS, SCIENCE

A Piece of the Earth

Celebrate Earth Day by helping your students create a "piece of the Earth" museum! Introduce the activity by sharing the poem "Who Am I?" (See page 10.) Explain that as "pieces of the Earth," we share our planet with many other natural objects such as rocks, flowers, leaves, and seashells. Send home a letter requesting that each child bring in a "piece of the Earth." Display the objects in the classroom on a table or bookshelf. Help children see the impact these objects have on our natural environment by creating a chart that lists each object, tells why it is important, and what would happen if it disappeared. Transfer this information to index cards to serve as museum notes for each object. Invite other classes to visit your museum, and let children take turns being tour guides.

Sue Frank
Frazier Elementary
Syracuse, New York

 **TIP**

Once you close the museum, use the objects for math activities such as counting, weighing, and sorting.

Name _____ Date _____

Who Am I?

The trees ask me,
And the sky,
And the sea asks me
     Who am I?

The grass asks me,
And the sand,
And the rocks ask me
     Who I am.

The wind tells me
At nightfall,
And the rain tells me
     Someone small.

Someone small
Someone small
But a piece
    of
    it
    all.

—Felice Holman

April Bubbles Chocolate:
An ABC of Poetry

Selected by Lee Bennett Hopkins (Simon & Schuster, 1994)

Organized in A–Z fashion, this anthology offers one poem for each letter of the alphabet. It includes work by well-known poets such as Charlotte Zolotow, Eve Merriam, Aileen Fisher, X. J. Kennedy, and Langston Hughes.

LANGUAGE ARTS, ART

A–Z Poetry

Create an alphabet book of poetry by collecting poems for each letter of the alphabet. Write each letter of the alphabet on a sheet of 11- by 18-inch (or larger) card stock. Add a cover and bind the pages together using loose-leaf binder rings (also called *O-rings*). Work with children to collect poems for the book in one of the following ways:

◎ Include poems by authors whose last names start with each letter of the alphabet.

◎ Include poems with one-word titles and arrange in alphabetical order, one poem per letter of the alphabet.

◎ Include favorite poems and arrange in the book according to the first letter of the first word in the title.

Copy each poem on the appropriate page. Let children take turns illustrating the poems. Share the book regularly by letting children take turns choosing a page to read. Make the book available for children to enjoy on their own and at home, too!

LANGUAGE ARTS

Pocket Poetry

Wouldn't it be nice to always have a "poem in your pocket"? Here's how you can have one handy to read in celebration of seasonal changes and special events in the classroom. Purchase a shoe organizer with several pockets. Label each pocket with a different category such as "Rainy Days," "Birthdays," "Lost Teeth," "Fall," or "New Students." Copy poems onto index cards that correspond to the categories you've selected and place them in the pockets. The next time someone loses a tooth or has a birthday, you'll be ready to celebrate with a "poem in your pocket"!

TIP

Let students add poems they have written to the class A-Z Poetry book!

MATH, LANGUAGE ARTS

Teaching With the Poster: "Poetry Time"

"It's poem o'clock, time for a rhyme…."
So begins the poem that will lead your students to establish a ritual for reading and enjoying poetry in the classroom this month and beyond!

Week One: A Poetry Place

Display the poetry poster and share it with students. Read it aloud together several times, then divide the class into three groups. Reread the poem, having each group read one of lines 3 to 5. Follow up by asking students to tell what they think happens during "poetry time." Work with them to establish a daily or weekly "poetry time" for the class. Set aside a special place to display related materials, such as:

- poems related to seasonal changes, current events, or units of study
- special-occasion poems (for birthdays, lost teeth, etc.)
- poems written by students; poems selected by students
- old favorites (poems children have heard several times before)
- poet studies (see Poet Tree, page 13)
- poems that lend themselves to music, movement, and instruments

Week Two: "Poem O'Clock"

Set an alarm clock each day, and when the alarm goes off, read the poster poem aloud, substituting the time for the words "poem o'clock." For example, say, "It's 10:15, time for a rhyme…." Share another poem with children at this time.

Week Three: Pocket Chart Poems

Write the words to the poster poem on sentence strips. In place of the words "poem o'clock," create strips with various times written digitally. Choose one of these strips and place it in the chart. Read the poem aloud with children. Ask for a volunteer to move the hands on an analog teaching clock to match the digital time in the pocket chart. Repeat the activity each day using different times.

Week Four: Taking Turns

Once children are familiar with the various Poetry Time routines, allow them to take turns leading the class in activities. Invite them to suggest new activities, too, and add these to the available choices.

Poet Tree

Who was Robert Frost? How about Langston Hughes? Introduce children to these poets and others by creating a Poet Tree. Begin by having children create a large tree on a bulletin board. Choose a favorite poet and gather pictures, information, and sample poems. Display the collection on the tree and share the poet's life and work with children. Change the tree regularly and involve students in your search for items to add to the display. Be sure to highlight a wide variety of poets with many different styles. Children will also enjoy using the Poet-Tree to highlight their own work. Share a few young poets each week to give everyone a chance to shine!

ComPuter Connection

For information on specific poets, click on the "Find a Poet" index at the Academy of American Poets web site.

www.poets.org/index/cfm

Teacher Share

LANGUAGE ARTS, ART

Off the Wall Poetry

Create a poetry-rich environment by posting poems on the walls of your school and classroom. Challenge children to search anthologies for poems that relate to objects or people found in your school. For example, "Band-Aids" by Shel Silverstein (*Where the Sidewalk Ends*, HarperCollins, 1974) could be hung outside the nurse's office, while "Table Manners" by Gelett Burgess (*Random House Book of Poetry*, Random House, 1983) would be appropriate in the cafeteria. Copy each poem on posterboard and let children add illustrations. Display the posters in the appropriate places around the school, and soon your walls will be alive with poetry!

Charlotte Sassman
Alice Carlson Applied Learning Center
Fort Worth, Texas

Book Break

Riddle Road: Puzzles in Poems and Pictures
by Elizabeth Spires (Margaret McElderry, 1999)

Tease and tantalize your students with this collection of 26 riddle poems. This book is the sequel to a first collection, *With One White Wing* (Margaret McElderry, 1995).

SCIENCE, LANGUAGE ARTS

Insect Riddle Poems

Kids love riddles and insects! By combining the two you'll have an activity they'll also love!

◎ Tell children that the poem you are about to read is a riddle poem. It is about an insect; however, the poet does not come out and tell you which one. Instead, she wants you to use the clues given in the poem to guess.

◎ Read the poem aloud. (See page 16.) Ask children to guess the insect. Once "firefly" is guessed, ask them to identify the clues that helped them to discover the subject of the poem.

◎ Let children create a collaborative riddle poem. Ask each child to write down the name of an insect on a slip of paper. Place the slips in a box and choose one at random. This will be the subject of your poem. Ask children to write down what comes to mind when they think of this insect. Elicit one word or phrase from each child, and record each response on a separate line on a sheet of chart paper. Title the poem "Who Am I?" and let the last line read, "Who am I?" Write the name of the insect next to the poem and cover it with a flap of paper. Write the words *I am a...* on the flap. Post the poem in the hallway for other students to enjoy.

◎ Encourage children to write their own riddle poems about other insects. Let them take turns sharing their poems with the class. Give students time to guess each insect's identity before letting the poet reveal the answer.

Book Break

Skip Across the Ocean: Nursery Rhymes From Around the World
collected by Floella Benjamin (Orchard Books, 1995)

This international collection of poetry includes verse from China, Nigeria, Peru, Sweden, Australia, and Greenland. In some cases, poems are written in both the original language and English.

Teacher Share

SCIENCE, LANGUAGE ARTS

Sensational Poetry

Spending time outdoors in the springtime can be a feast for children's senses as well as an inspiration to write poetry. Take your students on a quiet walk and encourage them to explore the outdoors using their senses. Invite them to record what they see, touch, smell, and hear in the spaces on a record sheet.(See sample, right.) Return to the classroom and let children write simple poems about spring using the following frame:

see 👁	touch ✋
ants clouds	flower petals bark
smell 👃	hear 👂
cut grass pine trees	birds

Welcome Spring!

I see _____

I hear _____

I smell _____

I touch _____

Spring is here!

Sue Lorey
Grove Avenue School
Barrington, Illinois

SOCIAL STUDIES, LANGUAGE ARTS

Fishing for Feelings

In order for children to express their feelings, they need to know the words associated with various emotions. In this bulletin board activity, children will learn this vocabulary and realize that behind every poem are the author's feelings.

Read "Poets Go Wishing" to children. (See page 17.) Explain that writing poetry is one way to express feelings, and that it's a poet's job to "fish" for the right words to match what they're feeling inside.

On the left side of a bulletin board, post a drawing of a child fishing. Brainstorm "feeling words" with children and write each one on a fish pattern. (See page 17.) Staple the fish to the bulletin board and title it "Poets Go Fishing."

As you interact with children, ask them to share how they're feeling, and encourage them to use the board as a resource to find the appropriate words.

TIP

For students who are familiar with basic "feeling words," extend the activity by choosing one word, and labeling a new set of fish with words or phrases that name other ways of telling about that feeling. For example, in the case of the word *excited*, students might volunteer *bursting with joy, bubbling,* or *jumping up and down.*

Name _____ Date _____

Have you ever watched a lighthouse
flashing in the dark?

Have you ever seen a flashlight
turning on and off?

Now think of something smaller
that blinks from dusk to dawn.

There I am! Catch me.
Catch me if you can.

firefly

—Elizabeth Spires

Fresh & Fun April Scholastic Professional Books
Reprinted with permission of Margaret K. McElderry Books, an imprint of Simon & Schuster Children's Publishing
Division from RIDDLE ROAD by Elizabeth Spires. Text copyright © 1999 by Elizabeth Spires.

Name _____ Date _____

Poets Go Wishing

Poets go fishing
with buckets
of words,
fishing
and wishing.

Using a line
that's loose or
tight
(Maybe this time
a rhyme is
right.)

Unreeling
unreeling
the words till they
match
the feeling the poet is
trying to
catch.

—Lilian Moore

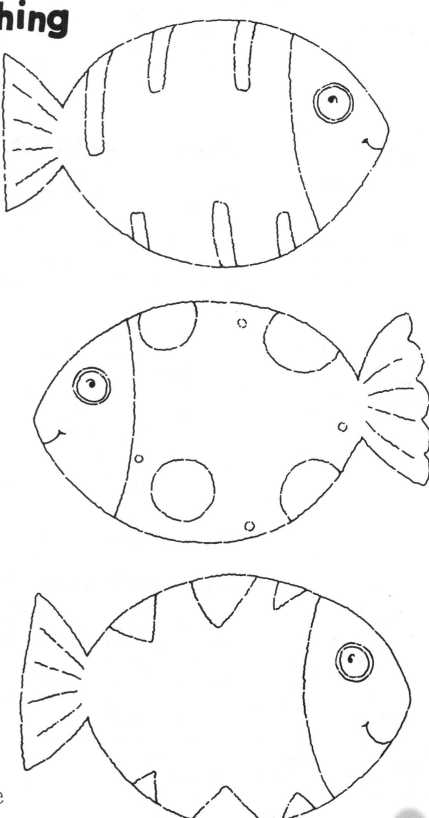

Little Cloud
by Eric Carle (Scholastic, 1996)

As Little Cloud moves through the sky, he changes into a sheep, an airplane, and two trees. Then he joins the other clouds and makes rain.

SCIENCE, ART

Cloud Parade Collaborative Banner

Take children outside on a day when there are lots of clouds in the sky. Invite them to lie on the grass and watch the "cloud parade." What pictures do they see in the sky? Back in the classroom, give children a sheet of white paper. Ask them to tear the paper into the shape of one of the pictures they saw during the "cloud parade," then paste it to light-blue construction paper. Have children copy each line of the following rhyme on their cloud pictures and complete the last sentence.

> Hooray for the cloud parade!
> Marching pictures through the sky.
> What will we see today?
> There goes a _____ floating by!

Create a cloud parade banner by gluing pictures side by side on a long sheet of banner paper. Display the banner up high so students can look up and watch the clouds go by!

TIP

Use the rhyme for a pocket chart activity. Copy the rhyme on sentence strips and place in the pocket chart. Give each child a piece of a sentence strip. Have children write the word for their cloud picture on the sentence strip. Read the rhyme aloud, again and again, letting children take turns completing the last sentence.

SCIENCE, LANGUAGE ARTS

Where Do Animals Go When It Rains?

As children participate in this rhyming play, they'll learn how animals seek shelter on rainy days. Organize the play in small groups as a Readers Theater or as a whole-class performance.

For Readers Theater, place children in groups of five. Assign each member of the group a different part and let children take turns reading aloud. To use the play as a whole-class activity, adapt the dialogue to reflect groups of squirrels, birds, spiders, and bees (rather than one of each). Choose one student to play the child, and divide the rest of the class into the four animal parts.

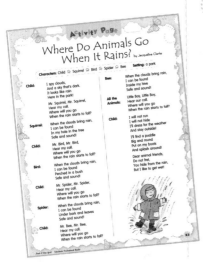

Teacher Share

MATH, SCIENCE

April Showers Calendar Activity

Is April really a rainy month? Present this research question on the last day of March (or as early in April as possible) and let students collect, record, and interpret weather data to find the answer. Make copies of the umbrella calendar squares (see right) and let students color and cut them out. As part of your calendar routine, ask children if there was any rain on the previous day. If the answer is *yes*, choose a student to tape an umbrella cutout to the calendar for that day. At the end of the month, restate the research question. Let students look at the data collected on the calendar to determine whether there were more days with or without rain in April.

Judy Meagher
Bozeman Schools
Bozeman, Montana

Umbrella Calendar
Cutout

SCIENCE

What Makes a Puddle?

Children love puddles! In this activity, they'll explore water and discover how puddles form.

◎ Give each child a sheet of waxed paper, a toothpick, an eyedropper, and a cup of water tinted with blue food coloring.

◎ Show children how to use their eyedropper to put five separate drops of water onto the waxed paper. Ask them to observe and describe the shape of the drops.

◎ Demonstrate how to pull one drop over to another. Ask children to describe what happened when the drops touched. Explain that this is how a puddle forms. Invite children to pull the rest of their drops over to the larger one. Ask: *How many drops make up your puddle?* Challenge children to pull the five drops out of the puddle. *Was it easy or difficult to pull each drop away? Did you pull out more or less than five drops?* Provide extra time for children to continue exploring the water. Ask them to share any observations they have made.

MOVEMENT, SCIENCE

Raindrop Relay

As children participate in this relay race, they'll follow a raindrop through the water cycle.

◎ Divide the class into two teams. Each team will need a set of three cones set up as shown, approximately eight feet apart. Use construction paper to label the cones "Puddle," "Cloud," and "Rain."

◎ Line up each team up behind the PUDDLE cone. Give the first player on each team a blue balloon on a string to represent a raindrop. On the word *Go*, the first player carries the raindrop from PUDDLE to CLOUD to RAIN and then back to PUDDLE. The next player in line then takes the raindrop and repeats the actions of the first player. The first team to get all its players through the water cycle wins the game!

SCIENCE

Absorb or Repel?

Have you ever noticed how rain rolls off an umbrella or raincoat? This is because nylon and rubber both repel water. In this activity, children test different kinds of materials to discover whether they absorb or repel.

◎ Place a sponge in a shallow tub. Ask children to predict whether it will absorb or repel water. Show them where to record their predictions on the record sheet. (See page 24.)

◎ Pour water over the sponge. Ask: *Did the water roll off or did the sponge soak it up?* Have children record the results on their record sheet. Repeat the activity using other objects, such as a paper towel, plastic wrap, soil, and a nylon or polyester sock.

◎ Once you've tested all the objects, ask children to examine the objects that absorbed water. Challenge them to place them in order from most to least absorbent. Continue to observe the objects periodically while they are drying. *Which object was the first to dry completely? the last?*

Book Break

Wonderful Worms

by Linda Glaser (Millbrook, 1994)

This informative book highlights the characteristics and contributions of the earthworm. Accompanying the simple text are illustrations that feature life above and below the ground in a garden.

SCIENCE, ART

Earthworm Mural

Why do worms come out when it rains? Post this question on a bulletin board or wall space in the hallway outside the classroom. Challenge children to use books and the Internet to find the answer. Have them create a mural to illustrate the answer. (*When worms' homes underground are flooded, they come out for air, which has been displaced by the water.*)

◎ Draw a line across the middle of a large sheet of craft paper to indicate ground level. Divide the class into two groups. Assign one group to illustrate the "aboveground" portion while the other does the "underground" scene.

◎ Have children record the answer to the question on chart paper or sentence strips and post this along with the mural in the hallway display. Children will take pride in sharing their knowledge with others, while fellow students and staff will enjoy learning something new!

TIP

Assist each group in brainstorming what the scene needs to include—for example, worms above ground and flooded passageways below ground.

Teacher Share

SOCIAL STUDIES, ART

Make a Rain Stick

Natives of the Amazon jungle believed they could coax water from the sky with rain sticks. Show children this location on a map and discuss the climate. Ask: *Why might these people need rain?* Let students make their own rain sticks. Give each child a cardboard tube from a roll of paper towels or gift wrap. Show children how to poke straight pins into the tube at equal distances, approximately every inch. Assist them in winding masking tape around the tube to secure the pins. Cut two 6-inch circles from the bottom of a grocery bag. Demonstrate how to place one circle over one end of the tube and secure it with a thick rubber band. Give each child a handful of rice. Have children pour the rice into their tubes and secure the open end with the remaining circle and a rubber band. Invite children to decorate their rain sticks with colorful patterns and designs. Let children experiment with using their rain sticks to create the sound of rain.

Bob Krech
Dutch Neck School
Princeton Junction, New Jersey

MUSIC, MOVEMENT

Let's Make Rain!

Lead children in the following movements to simulate a rainstorm.
Make each sound for five to ten seconds:

- Slide palms back and forth.
- Tap fingers together.
- Snap fingers.
- Clap hands.
- Slap thighs.
- Stomp feet.

- Slap thighs.
- Clap hands.
- Snap fingers.
- Tap fingers together.
- Slide palms back and forth.
- Rest hands quietly in lap.

Teacher Share

LANGUAGE ARTS, SCIENCE

Move Like Water

Watch children move through the water cycle with this interactive poem.

Surprise!

I'm a puddle. Splash me!	(stamp feet up and down)
I'm water vapor. Watch me rise!	(squat with arms around knees and slowly stand up)
I'm in a cloud, Condensing.	(pull arms into chest) (students huddle together)
I'm raining down.	(stand with arms overhead— wiggle fingers and lower body down)
SURPRISE!	(jump up)

Natalie Vaughn
Phoenix School
Encinitas, California

Where Do Animals Go When It Rains?
by Jacqueline Clarke

Characters: Child 🌧 Squirrel 🌧 Bird 🌧 Spider 🌧 Bee   **Setting:** a park

Child:
I spy clouds,
And a sky that's dark.
It looks like rain
Here in the park!

Mr. Squirrel, Mr. Squirrel,
Hear my call.
Where will you go
When the rain starts to fall?

Squirrel:
When the clouds bring rain,
I can be found
In my hole in the tree
Safe and sound!

Child:
Mr. Bird, Mr. Bird,
Hear my call.
Where will you go
When the rain starts to fall?

Bird:
When the clouds bring rain,
I can be found
Perched in a bush
Safe and sound!

Child:
Mr. Spider, Mr. Spider,
Hear my call.
Where will you go
When the rain starts to fall?

Spider:
When the clouds bring rain,
I can be found
Under bark and leaves
Safe and sound!

Child:
Mr. Bee, Mr. Bee,
Hear my call.
Where will you go
When the rain starts to fall?

Bee:
When the clouds bring rain,
I can be found
Inside my hive
Safe and sound!

All the Animals:
Little Boy, Little Boy,
Hear our call.
Where will you go
When the rain starts to fall?

Child:
I will not run
I will not hide
I'll dress for the weather
And stay outside!

I'll find a puddle
Big and round
Put on my boots
And splash around!

Dear animal friends,
Do not fret,
You hide from the rain,
But I like to get wet!

Name _____ Date _____

Absorb or Repel?

Object	My Prediction		Results	
	Absorb	Repel	Absorb	Repel
1				
2				
3				
4				
5				
6				

Teacher Share

Who's Hiding? Mini-Book

Use this repetitive mini-book to give your students practice reading and to introduce them to a variety of animals that hatch from eggs.

◎ Make one book for each child by folding two sheets of 8- by 11-inch paper into four sections and cutting on the folds. Give each child a copy of the riddles on page 30. Ask children to cut out the egg-shaped riddles. Show them how to glue down just the tip of each egg to create one flap per page (excluding the front and back covers). Have children add a front and back cover, and staple the pages together.

◎ Read each riddle aloud with children. See if they can guess the animal's name. Ask them to tell you which clues helped them to figure out the answer. Invite them to use crayons or markers to draw a picture of that animal under the flap. Repeat these steps with the remaining riddles.

◎ Give children time to practice reading their mini-books with partners. Let them take the books home to share with their families, too.

Natalie Vaughn
Phoenix School
Encinitas, California

TIP

Answers, clockwise from the top left of the activity page are: *caterpillar, penguin, sea turtle, ostrich, frog, chick.*

Out Popped a....

You'll get a surprise every time with this interactive rhyme! Prepare for the activity by sending each child home with a plastic egg. Ask children to place something inside (either an object or a picture) that wouldn't ordinarily hatch from an egg. Tell them the sillier the better!

Copy the rhyme at right onto chart paper or sentence strips. When children return to school with their eggs, teach them the rhyme. Let them take turns reading the rhyme aloud and filling in the blanks. When they get to the first blank, they should name an adjective that describes their egg. When they complete the second blank, they should open their egg to reveal what's hidden inside.

I went for a walk
and what did I find?
A _____ egg,
someone left behind.

It started to crack
before my eyes.
Out popped a _____ .
What a surprise!

Internet Egg Hunt

How many eggs does a swan lay? How about a frog? Give each child (or partners) a copy of the Internet Egg Hunt. (See page 31.) Challenge children to search the web to find out how many eggs each animal lays. When a child finds an answer, invite him or her to share it with the rest of the class so everyone can record it on their sheets. Talk about which animal lays the most eggs and which lays the least. Happy hunting!

SCIENCE, MATH

How Big Is This Egg?

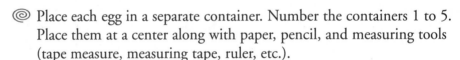

Which animal lays the biggest egg? the smallest? In this activity, children measure and compare five different animal eggs.

◉ Make five eggs out of clay, using the following dimensions as a guide. (These are in mm—25 mm per inch.)

Ostrich: 175 X 145   **Platypus:** 18 X 15
Chicken: 50 X 30   **Hummingbird:** 12 X 8
Pigeon: 40 X 24

◉ Place each egg in a separate container. Number the containers 1 to 5. Place them at a center along with paper, pencil, and measuring tools (tape measure, measuring tape, ruler, etc.).

◉ Invite children to visit the center and measure the length and circumference of each egg. Have them record the measurements.

◉ On the chalkboard, list the animals that go with the eggs. Challenge children to match each egg with an animal. After sharing the answers with children, ask them if they think the size of an animal has anything to do with the size of the egg it lays. Have them explain their answers.

TIP

Challenge children to find egg sizes for other animals. Dinosaur eggs, for example, ranged in size from a grain of rice to bigger than a bowling ball!

Book Break

Chickens Aren't the Only Ones
by Ruth Heller (Paper Star, 1999)

Written in verse, this book shows readers that frogs, snails, spiders, and even platypus lay eggs.

Teacher Share

SCIENCE

How Are These Animals Alike?

Color and cut out pictures of animals that lay eggs, such as those pictured here. Fold them in half and place each inside a plastic egg. One by one, have students "crack" the eggs. After they open all the eggs, ask children to tell you what the animals have in common. Explain that these animals are all *oviparous*, which means they produce eggs that hatch outside the body. Challenge students to name other animals that hatch eggs. Let them draw and label new pictures to put inside the eggs.

Mary Rosenberg
Kratt Elementary School
Fresno, California

MATH

Egg Count Math Story Mat

As children manipulate jelly bean eggs between two bird's nests, they'll gain practice in counting, addition, and equal shares. Prepare by giving each child a copy of the math story mat (see page 32) and 20 jelly beans. Guide them in using the jelly beans as manipulatives to find the answer to the following story problems:

◎ Place three eggs in the robin's nest and five eggs in the blue jay's nest. Which nest has more eggs? How many more eggs are in the blue jay's nest? (Repeat as needed, substituting different numbers.)

◎ Place five eggs in the robin's nest and four eggs in the blue jay's nest. How many eggs are in the nests all together? Can you find a different way to show nine eggs? (Repeat as needed, substituting different numbers.)

◎ Using eight eggs, give each bird an equal share. (Repeat as needed, substituting different numbers.)

SCIENCE

Breathing Room

In this experiment, children will discover that an eggshell has tiny holes in it so air can reach the animal growing inside. Place an egg in a jar half-filled with warm water. Ask: *Does the egg sink or float?* Have students observe the bubbles coming from the egg. What do they tell us? (*The eggshell is* porous—*it has holes in it—so air can go in or out of the egg.*) Discuss why it is important for an eggshell to have holes in it. (*to provide air to the baby growing inside*)

Book Break

Look Who's Hatching!
by the World Wildlife Fund (Cedco Publishing, 1998)

As children turn the cutaway pages or lift the flaps of this book, they'll reveal baby animals whose nests can be found in logs, sandy holes, and riverbanks.

Teacher Share

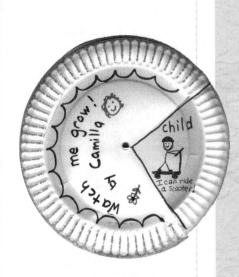

SCIENCE

Watch Me Grow!

Children create life cycle wheels to reflect on the past, present, and future.

◎ Give each child two paper plates and a brass fastener. Assist children in using a pencil and ruler to divide one plate into four equal sections. Have children label the sections with the four stages of life: *baby, child, adult,* and *senior citizen,* then draw pictures or paste photos of themselves at each stage.

◎ Demonstrate how to cut out one section from the second paper plate. Help children push the brass fastener through the center of the two paper plates (with the life cycle wheel on the bottom). Children can turn the bottom plate to share their life cycle with classmates, friends, and family.

Sandy Hoff, Heather Kurtenbach, Stephanie Bushjahn
Dakota State University
Madison, South Dakota

MUSIC, MOVEMENT

From Caterpillar to Butterfly

As children act out the life cycle of a butterfly, they'll learn what happens at each stage of metamorphosis. You'll need a sleeping bag and a brightly colored beach towel.

Demonstrate how to move through the life cycle, using the movements and props described. (See right.)

Let each child take a turn. Extend the activity by letting children come up with ways to act out the life cycle of a frog and chicken.

Stage	Movement
Egg	scrunch body into a ball
Larva	crawl across the floor
Pupa	crawl into the sleeping bag
Adult	pop out of the sleeping bag wearing butterfly wings (beach towel)

SNACK

Edible Nests

Tell children they should never touch a nest if it is still home to a family of birds. Then, follow this recipe to create bird's nests children can not only touch, but also eat! (Note: The following recipe makes about 20 nests.)

◉ Melt 1 stick margarine in a large saucepan over low heat. Add a 10-ounce bag of large marshmallows and stir until melted. Turn off the heat and stir in 12 crumbled shredded wheat biscuits.

◉ After the mixture has cooled slightly, place 1 tablespoon of the warm mixture on a sheet of waxed paper for each child. Let children shape the mixture into a bird's nest.

◉ When the nests are completely cool, add a few jelly bean "eggs."

TIP

Check for food allergies before serving the edible nests.

MOVEMENT, SCIENCE

Chicken Dance

As children create movements to go with the following song, they'll explore the "dance" that chickens do as they hatch from eggs.

Once students memorize the song, ask them to come up with movements for each line. Sing the song several times using the children's movements.

I'm a Little Chicken
(sung to "I'm a Little Teapot")

I'm a little chicken,
Ready to hatch,
Pecking at my shell,
Scratch, scratch, scratch.
When I crack it open, out I'll leap,
Fluff up my feathers and cheep, cheep, cheep!

by Susan Peters

Who's Hiding? Mini-Book

This baby's so tiny,
It would fit in a spoon.
Before it grows up,
It'll spin a cocoon.

This baby keeps warm
On its daddy's feet.
It will be black and white
And have fish to eat.

This baby is yellow,
And covered with fluff.
It pecks at the ground
'Til it's eaten enough.

This baby has flippers
And swims very well.
It doesn't have teeth
And carries a shell.

This swimmy baby
Will get a surprise.
It'll grow four long legs
And eat lots of flies.

This baby's eggs
Are the biggest around.
It has two small wings,
But can't leave the ground.

Name _____ Date _____

Internet Egg Hunt

Animal	Number of Eggs
① Swan	
② Woodpecker	
③ Lizard	
④ Frog	
⑤ Turtle	

◎ Which animal lays the most eggs? _____

◎ Which animal lays the fewest eggs? _____

Fresh & Fun April Scholastic Professional Books

Egg Count Math Story Mat

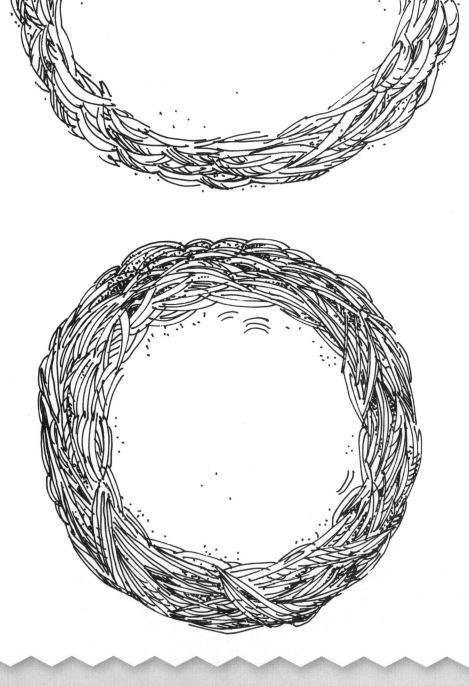

Fresh & Fun April   Scholastic Professional Books